evolution

Also by Eileen Myles

Afterglow (a dog memoir)

I Must Be Living Twice: New and Selected Poems 1975–2014

Snowflake / different streets

Inferno (a poet's novel)

The Importance of Being Iceland / travel essays in art

Sorry, Tree

Tow (with drawings by artist Larry R. Collins)

Skies

on my way

Cool for You

School of Fish

Maxfield Parrish / early & new poems

The New Fuck You / adventures in lesbian reading (with Liz Kotz)

Chelsea Girls

Not Me

1969

Bread and Water

Sappho's Boat

A Fresh Young Voice from the Plains

Polar Ode (with Anne Waldman)

The Irony of the Leash

evolution

eileen myles

Grove Press

New York

Text Design by Norman E. Tuttle of Alpha Design & Composition
This book is set in 12 pt. Bembo by Alpha Design & Composition
of Pittsfield, NH

First Grove Atlantic hardcover edition: September 2018

Published simultaneously in Canada
Printed in the United States of America

FIRST EDITION

ISBN 978-0-8021-2850-8
eISBN 978-0-8021-4636-6

Library of Congress Cataloguing-in-Publication data
is available for this title.

Grove Press
an imprint of Grove Atlantic
154 West 14th Street
New York, NY 10011
Distributed by Publishers Group West
groveatlantic.com

18 19 20 21   10 9 8 7 6 5 4 3 2 1

for Adam Fitzgerald

contents

evolution

I am Ann Lee. I thought that would be a good place to start. I am Eileen Myles. I am 67 years old. My mother died on April 3rd. She was 96. I have not had sex since January. I am writing to you from Cape Cod. It was a horrible week. It was kind of a stray week. I really wanted to be home in New York and I had just gotten back from three weeks in Palestine, Ukraine and Russia. I resisted the impulse to say "the Ukraine." Is that its name. I just wanted to be home after that. I had planned to be in Provincetown in August but there was this available week in June. I thought that'd be nice. Yeah but won't you be tired. You know that thing where you know something but you speed up over that voice convincing yourself that the logical thing is true. I came up here with a friend and we did a little work together and next morning she got on one of those tiny planes. We thought this is such a Sagittarian trip that she would drive up to the Cape with me & my dog to do a little work and leave the next morning in order to hear a band named red ants spelled red aunts that she really loves and they were after all really great. I began my week of relaxing and working and being in my home state. I began to miss my mom. Around weather. Because it was horrible this week. It like rained all day long and all night long. I didn't have to go to the beach but you know it was cold too and I was staying in an unheated shack in a part of Provincetown called Tasha Hill which is very rustic which means wet wood and hobbit houses and goats and horses and roaming dogs and chipmunks but like really chilly and the internet wasn't working and the gas wasn't on and using the space heater I blew a fuse. It's a *circuit* corrected Thomas who I rented the place from. Who cares, it blew, it blew. It rained and rained and I wanted to call my mother in her nursing home in Greenfield and say what do you think of this weather. And she would say it stinks. But I can't. That's exactly the way I miss my mother. A deepening of the abyss with a hoot. I miss that. I mean there were many nice moments including one last night when it was already nice again and I was stepping over a wall onto the wooden ladder onto the beach and I thought I'm like Tennessee Williams. I'm like an old queer in the winter in Provincetown waiting for Marlon Brando to come down and fix the pipes and then prove to be the right one to play Stanley in Streetcar Named Desire. I did a little bit of research. Ann Lee thought that she was the church. Get it an edifice. And that is a radical thought. Not being cast as a thing. The live woman expanding out. Jesus was the church and she was the church. She was the second coming and now god was complete being both woman and man. It's so important that she had those four miscarriages and never proved to lay an egg correctly and convinced her blacksmith husband to not lay eggs with her. People chuckle when you say Shakers when you remind them they were celibate. How did they reproduce. Well they adopted. They recruited. Found-lings! There were indentured Shakers I read which I am waiting for someone to explain the relationship between economic servitude and Shakerhood. The fact that you don't have to breed to survive is inspiring to me. Or maybe it's you won't have to die. Right away. Ann Lee could have kept trying and one of those pregnancies might have made a baby and one of them would kill her. Not now. She said lifting a hand. I won't survive but my church will. My work. That it was thought up or furthered by a woman who was not barren or infertile but generative. I am Eileen I am not celibate. I'm sort of between relationships and I've had sex a few times in the gap but I

2

had a bit of that feeling of who is this for so I thought that's no way to go ahead. I love that the place where the Shakers landed in this reproductive, no, productive, generative scheme—is the thought to make things and make things well. It's such a beautiful thought. I won't dwell on my own sexuality too much but I do want to say I love the idea of making something with another human being, perhaps me, not a baby but something nice. A special place perhaps. But for now I'm loving the solo place of the life well made. I thought well I was walking on the beach and I thought what about one blue stone and I picked it up. I've had all this crap in my pockets tokens of this and that and I'm ready to whittle it down and examine my own message and my own time. I'm holding this rock with that thought.

Did you watch Comey. People were like is he hot. I mean I don't know. He's beautiful unbeautiful like those boys I went to grade school with. The big bags under his eyes. To his credit HE did not make the joke about dinner with Trump being the all-time great excuse for breaking a date with your wife. That was the other guy. Yet he smirked because he was a man and a man has to get the other man's joke or else it's a cause for violence. But in that moment typically there was a woman pushed out thoughtlessly like a buffoon. Aren't we all looking for an excuse to get away from her. But where are you going. To sit in this room. Do you remember when he talked about justice with a blindfold over her eyes. I realized at that moment that I had never wondered who put the blindfold on. It's a construction. Whose? In his own defense Comey said she did not lift her blindfold and peek to see if her patron was pleased. I thought of that as a trans vernacular moment. Code shifting. I mean just before various speakers had been peppering their questions in this mostly male gathering, America's Congress with their photographer and journalist friends, they peppered their talk with a number of "heck of a"s and gosh just to say that despite being suits they were manly men, trusty doers, and representatives of a doing nation, which we are not of course, so all these conceits to present ourselves as manly are drag of course, but my point is that when this tall man depicts his own relationship to justice the higher authority to whom he has dedicated his life he depicts her as she is historically depicted as the woman who has mysteriously had her sight taken away AND if HE were to degrade his lofty position he would do it coquettish-like, taking a peek like a girl. And that is only possible that rhetorical turn because justice has been presented as female—made wholly useful as a symbol, incomplete, because she is blinded by men. Male rhetoric would not work without the fall guy of woman. In the constructed absence of women we make lies. That's what America makes.

Now the president I think the imputation was he was actually trying to feminize our guy and get him to lift that blinder and see if Donald was smiling at him or not. Comey was appealing to their masculine pride. Was *he* liking him now. Was Comey serving at his pleasure. There's so much weird gender stuff in this largely government as men by men for men. If women are only a symbol then men may lie. When Trump asked Comey at the dinner table to do naughty things like take a loyalty oath to him and not to the blinded girl he gave vague answers back to him. The congressmen who questioned Comey asked well why why didn't you tell him this was inappropriate. I I was stunned was Comey's reply.

Let's pause for a second. Doesn't this sound like every rape case you've ever heard. And doesn't the questioner normally barge in hard at that moment. You were STUNNED. I have a dictionary definition of the term stunned. Were you drugged. Did he hit you with his raygun. Everyone laughs. That did not happen. Because this is not a real girl. This is a feint. All the guys are in on the play. The audacity of the situation—a man presented by himself to all who already know him as such a one of high purpose and then been treated so cavalierly by this thug of a president—that is tantamount to an insult to all of us of course. Honest men. We're going to see the stuff America is made of. We're going to see how our democracy works! I was walking down Commercial Street with my dog holding my phone listening to this important testimony yesterday as Comey talked about his loyalty to the department of Justice and to the FBI for which he would be grateful all his life and tears came to my eyes. Notice this I thought. Why am *I* getting tearful. Who put this in me. Ann Lee proposed herself to be a church. Was I roofied. Is that why I cry. James Comey said that America was a shining city on a hill. Now that's insane. What hill. He said that this was not a republican issue or democratic issue – he was talking about hacking now, about the Russians trying to hack our election. And nobody yet has mentioned that there was a female candidate who was robbed right in front of all of us of her rightful place of office as the president of the united states. I think because it wasn't done to a man, it was done to a woman. Not having managed to land herself in the seat, she remains symbolic. He said I don't THINK Russians ARE democrats or republicans and everyone laughed. The joke of course hid the lie in what he just said. The Russians were of course hacking on behalf of the Republican party or Donald Trump. When Trump asked Comey to go easy on Flynn, when he asked him to dispel this cloud around me, the Russian stuff, he admitted it was POSSIBLE that some of his SATELLITES might've talked to the Russians. Satellite is the word we need. Either Russia is a satellite of the Republican party or the Republican party is a satellite of Russia. That's the dance. [Arm bar movement.] I love the Shaker thing about dancing. Will there be any of that this weekend. It seemed circular, it seemed like hands were raised at crucial times and sometimes people would go wig out for an ecstatic solo. Think about dancing. We have lost our rituals and we need them. I mean dancing was never so intense in my life as it was in junior high and high school really before I was having sex and you would feel this tremendous excitement in the watching and coordination and collective unh and bliss. The repression enabled I'll speak for myself me to really cut loose. In New York in the 70s and 80s there was a free-floating loft party a dancing party called the loft and it would gather in lofts on special appointed nights there was probably a mailing list and mythic deejaying took off there, it changed the form, and numerous dance styles and merging of avant garde and disco and Buddhist chant (Arthur Russell) and people would just pulsate and sweat and it was very much a religion. I went once in the hey day like thirty years ago and then I went again it still happens the night before Thanksgiving you know we had just had this election and dancing seemed like the only cure and the party was in a small basement of a club in Brooklyn very interracial very all ages and there was an intuitive sharing of space. It was such a political thing. Late in the night a bunch of white rich kids descended on us the trumps I thought as they were extremely high and looked kind of grotesque they were dancing at you mocking the act of dancing even and pleasure and it felt violent as they took extra awkward even square space real estatey and you just felt pushed and I left. I went home. I had to get up early and go see my mother.

Did you ever watch the show The OA. I really recommend it. Netflix. The reason I mention it here is that it's sort of about a cult that arises among a group of kidnapped people looking for a way out and their leader is this formerly blind woman who discovers her sight through dreams, and she begins to construct a way for her small community in adjoining glass cages by means of a choreography also discovered by her in dreams which will one by one liberate the dancers. The thing is you have to die. It's the dreams you have while you're dying. And there was some mechanism through which their captor would make each of them go through near death for his own purposes. Everyone was looking for something down there. Though the girl was originally from Russia and it was there that she lost her

sight she travelled to America searching for her father and got kid-
napped instead. But she became a leader inside as prisoners often do.

I have a bunch of poems I thought I might read you and also
maybe two different well are they essays . . . one is a speech that I
wrote for an event just before the election on the highline and it
was organized around Zoe Leonard's "I want a dyke for president"
broadside which was posted I don't know how many feet high out-
side, and her piece was inspired in fact by *my* own actually campaign
as a dyke for president of the united states in 1992. Zoe said maybe
you would like to update your campaign somehow. Yeah I thought.
I would like to win. So I wrote that. And we honestly all thought
Hillary was going to win at that moment and I DON'T presume
that you all supported her. I did. I do presume like me you might
believe that what we had in November was a coup. And that was
what brought me here to the Feminine Mystic.[1] It was the excel-
lent invitation. Perhaps you agree with me that it was uncannily
possible for us to have an open coup d'etat in America because the
candidate was a woman. Not an American tried and true. Useful. A
sewer of flags. Bake cookies, bake cookies. Perhaps someone who
refuses to sit at the back of the bus and starts a revolution that way.
Perhaps a claimer that I am a church, female head of a cult that
invented clothespins and shared their inventions without patents like
Native Americans sharing the sky and the land. What Comey said
that enraged me the most is that he was outraged that the Russians
would tamper with our electoral process. Our shining shitty on
the hill. Anyone here could probably tell me how many countries
have legally elected socialist presidents, and moderate presidents and
communist presidents and much revered and inspiring presidents
and our government in response utterly disregarding their electoral

1. You are reading a talk I gave at a conference in June 2017, The Feminine Mystic,
co-sponsored by Shaker Museum | Mount Lebanon and Bard College at Simon's
Rock

process funded a right-wing autocrat, a monarchist, a human-rights violator who would make a deal. I don't know if we are the most corrupt nation on earth. Does it need to start there? It's just that having taken the land from one people and then dragged another people from their continent to work on it for free and then deciding that you want California and Texas and Montana and Idaho and New Mexico and Arizona so you take that from another people I mean when I think that Los Angeles was a Mexican city in 1848. We just thought we would take it. And our soldiers went into Veracruz raping people. Just cause they could. And now we're going to build a wall. James Comey is not the gentleman and Donald Trump is the barbarian. James Comey knows (everything I just said) and that's the monstrosity. It's just that James Comey can make me get teary-eyed like parades used to do cause I wanted to march and I never did. I guess I did once. I was in a group called ILGO—Irish Lesbian and Gay Organization. And they were chiefly about getting the Ancient Order of Hibernians to allow us to march in the St. Patrick's Day Parade. I didn't know it could matter so much. I never realized how outside I was until I realized they wouldn't let me in. They didn't want me. I didn't know. I just thought I was weird.

Once in the 80s I was on West 16th Street at a meeting at a church called St. Francis Xavier which was a cool church that would lay out the cots for the homeless after we left. But that night there was a candlelit procession going around sixth avenue down fifteenth street up fifth ave and up sixteenth again and the reason they were marching was that the cardinal of New York had just decided that Dignity the gay catholic group could no longer meet in catholic community spaces in all the boroughs of New York. Because of aids activism mainly. He was like *oh yeah*. Look what I can do.

I'm an ex catholic. Why would I care, but I stood there sobbing watching those women and men holding the orange candles as a symbol no a fact of their unvanquished pride. At the St Patrick's day march I stood along the side of the parade pointing I think at the police shouting Shame Shame Shame. I guess because I have spent so much of my life feeling ambivalent about where I am, the institutions that bred me, the ways when I was younger I had to do insanely boring things to make money, the ways as a woman I was shocked at the things men said to me, that people of greater privilege said to me, that when I have an unambivalent feeling about wanting to take part in something, to blindly say yes, to yell something, to feel awe at a natural spectacle, to hear only the music I'm hearing the speech that I'm listening to dance when I'm dancing, to enjoy walking my dog, when I feel inside my life and any and any of its features I feel grateful and stunned. And I want to tell you about it. Because to be living in a country that has been actively constructing a lie for its entire history, and this most recent chapter is, I can't help it, the most startling to me yet. If I was awake when Fred Hampton was shot in his bed by the FBI it might have mattered then. But in that whole hearing yesterday nobody went, but wait we're not talking about in the abstract a future election that could be hacked. It happened. It already happened. And that requires us to be here. Now. No place else and it's the hardest place in the world. Like I think Comey knows, they all know but if they don't, if what we're watching is a twelve step program of dishonesty then they are the stepford wives. And it's always like that. Everything is the reverse. They are asleep and we are awake. They are weak and we are strong. Not because I am female but because I have the other in me. I am awake to feel that. Obviously I fail . . .

I shouldn't have done this, I'm glad I did that. Do you do that. I want to get better. I want to feel awake all the time. I got asked to be the keynote here I thought of course. *Feminine Mystic Shakers*. It all adds up. In this climate, with this blue stone in my hand I must be here. I shouldn't have gone to Russia. It was great but I didn't really need to go. I absolutely am glad I went to Palestine. Let me witness some of that. Again I felt unlikely. I met someone in Texas who had just edited a book about writers on Palestine and we just liked each other. Ru Freeman is her name. So I'm in Boston for a month doing some residency. She asks me to come to New York and be on a panel in a bookstore about the book even though I'm not in it. I went. I couldn't stop myself. I thought why am I doing this. Sitting on the train crazy and tired. And I thought most of the people in the room in New York couldn't figure out why I was there. I was likening rent stabilized apartments in New York to Palestine. And you know it was true. I went back to Boston and like a year later I'm invited to Palestine. And it was amazing. It was just like my landlord. You know much worse. The goal in Palestine is ethnic cleansing. To get Palestinians out of the Jewish state. If you go to college outside of Palestine you can't come home. If you go to college in Palestine you might get kidnapped. There's a glass wall on the campus in Jerusalem the Israeli army keeps knocking down just for the fuck of it. They steal computers out of the labs. I mean these are like hot teenagers boys and girls with machine guns. We must understand kids. Youth. We must not send them to war. To die. To kill. I met a woman who was born in Canada. She lives in Ramallah now. She only knew her family was from Nazareth. Where's that. She learned that her father's younger brother was shot by a member of the IDF. With that he got out of there as quickly as he could with his family and never mentioned what had happened. Now that woman is a writer and a lawyer who specializes in demolitions. Obviously if you want people to leave you destroy their homes. Do you know any martyrs I asked her. I thought it must be local, it must be true. I had never been there before. Not in this life. Not on this planet. That's why I'm telling you all this. She said she knew of this kid who was 17 or 18 and he was from a refugee family so the girl he wanted to marry's family didn't want her getting involved. Refugee=underclass. Worldwide right. Then I think he didn't get into college. And then his friend was shot by the Israeli army. So. He strapped a bomb to himself and walked into a beauty parlor and blew it up. His family was devastated. Had no idea of this plan, the extent of his suffering. And their home of course was demolished. You can't be there and see the settlements perched on the mountaintops and the hills terraced with Palestinian trees and flocks of sheep and roads built up the mountain that not only can the Palestinians not use, but their own roads are destroyed and what used to take ten minutes now takes an hour and there are checkpoints so it could be five hours or six hours. You could never get home.

If you saw this you would not be able to abide this suffering so you must not see it.

Comey says please don't let me be alone with him again to Sessions about Trump and Pence can't be alone with a woman other than his wife. Men fear predation widely.

I have the other in me so I don't fear women or men.

I love this quote from Édouard Glissant, the Martinique poet & philosopher. No first this quote from someone else who "defined the utopia as something that's missing."[2] We must be there. If it isn't here we have to make it.

This is Glissant.

I think that utopia, in the end, for me, would be this force that is the opposite of power. This force that each of us has to be able to approach, intuit, touch, seize upon the inextricable of the world. And for that, there are no privileged classes. I say: we are all young before the world. And this youth, it's the capacity to feel all the world's flows mixing together, mixing together in a completely unexpected and completely inextricable way. Utopia is the force of feeling this.[3]

---

2. From a conversation between Adorno and Ernest Bloch

3. From *Mondialité: Or the Archipelagos of Édouard Glissant*

When I walked into my mother's room on Thanksgiving she said you're late. I'm not, I said. And I wasn't. I'm always late but I arrived earlier. She must be confused. I had flowers. Here Mum. Oh why did you do that. She seemed genuinely troubled. You love flowers mom. Oh. Then I sat down. I was a little uncomfortable. I was so far from my mother. Across the room. We were going to have dinner downstairs. She heard they had a good spread. Next to me on the teevee table was Frosty. My aunt Anne, my mother's sister, used to take a ceramics class. She had made this Frosty the snowman with a black top hat and see-through multicolored buttons down his belly that lit when you plugged it in. My sister who was the keeper of my mother's things and things in general had just brought Frosty out for the holiday. I pulled my chair forward and I had to tug a little bit because it was attached to something and then I heard a crash. It was Frosty. Oh no. Look what you've done. Finally I had failed and I felt like my mother liked that. Each person from the nursing home coming in to clean up made it worse. Oh, Frosty they said. Oh no. That's sad.

I began picking the pieces up. I put them in an empty coffee cup and took it home. Forget it my mother said. No I'm going to fix it. Frosty sat on my kitchen counter for a couple of weeks. I had gorilla glue and I was doing an awkward job and it looked bad. I was out with some friends at dinner and I told them the story and they laughed and laughed especially about the bad job I was doing. You should ask Andrew. Andrew? You know Andrew who makes ceramics. It was true. I hadn't seen him in years. Do you have his number. He's on facebook.

I explained the situation and Andrew instructed me to go to a sculptor's shop in Manhattan to pick up some special clay. I brought it to his studio in Bushwick. He had an assistant there who seemed sweet and not entirely convinced he should be there. Angel. I think that was his name. Andrew paced and gleamed up at me. I think this should be no problem. In about a week. He looked up smiling at me. Great.

I saw my mother as herself one more time. She was very sleepy. Frosty stood guard in a new Eileen-proof position in the room. Hey Frosty looks good I said. I couldn't resist. Yeah my mother said as if she were already doing much better things in the world.

When I saw her again she was asleep all the time. She had had a major stroke right after lunch. It was weird because she had been doing well and was even going to leave the nursing home and move in with my sister and her partner. People never leave the nursing home. Yeah but her heart changed that.

I was with her for five days. She was lying there with her mouth open snoring. I thought of high school when I would stay up watching late night teevee with her and my brother and she would fall asleep and we would laugh at her snoring. It was the exact same thing. We were awake and she was tired from her day.

I came in one morning and it was cold outside. She really wasn't communicating at all. The nurses would say do you want this. Does that feel bad, does that feel okay and she would nod yes or no. I put my hands on her as soon as I entered the room. Ooh Frosty she said, almost flirting which was my mother's way. My siblings looked horrified, and those I'm sure were her very last words.

Evolution

Something
unearthly
about
today
so I buy
a Diet Coke &
a newspaper
a version of "me"
something
about me on the
earth & its sneakers
& feeling like
the earth's furniture
but that can't be
true or like
the coke & the Times
it's true for a little
while. I'm not
the earth's furniture
not entirely &
I seem to want
to go about this

in the entirely
wrong way. My face
asks the
man at the deli
do you know
me & he clearly
didn't answer
me enough
I'll get this
I said
picking up the
paper hoping
that he just
might know
me a little
bit more but
not enough to make
me feel ab
solutely true. I'm
just not true
enough so it's
probably the weather
an overripe
September & we're
agreeing that
the winter
will probably be
pretty cold. That feels
good & true

I thought talking
to Jill who is
my trainer. She shows
me what to do
& I feel a little
better after that
and I thought I don't
want to be like
that poet I thought
he's just like a
prisoner of the planet
& that's what's
sad about him. I could
say unlike me who is
like a temporary
chair but I'm
actually what's
on the chair. I'm
using this pen
on a purple notebook
set up on the
angle of my
thighs. My thighs.
I've had you since
I was a kid.
I've known you for so
long. Even when
you betrayed
me in the bathtub

one night when
you were rabbits
but that's cause
I was going
crazy. Is it crazy
to be the
citizen who's
only partially
here. Like
kissing while
your eyes
anxiously are surveying
the room. Kissing
at a party
but there's nobody
there but this
person with not
so many characteristics
and she will list
them so she can
continue writing.
That's what I
like about
this act. The sea
of blood & consciousness
& barely repressed
craziness that's
singing in my
ears only

likes one thing
always like
her favorite
food. The gulls
in my head
can do whatever
they want
and I can't
ever use
a wrong word
at the
right time &
this is
it when
the earth
only wants me
this way
ignoring
the seagulls
and writing.

I could
stop here
cause the
coke is
so good
I want
to go further
longer. Where

should I
go. My foot scrapes
against
a book
wondering. Today
I discovered
that to
talk about
certain
things makes
me sad.
So I'll stop.
There. My arm rests
on a pillow &
that feels
pretty good. I cherish
this time alone.
When I go
out I think
why am I
here. I'd like to change
the very
characters
I'm writing
in. If I could
stop
thinking
about _if_
you know

me what
else
could I do.
I could
go to the
movies
but afterwards
it would be
me talking
about what was
so obviously
wrong. And now
I'm picking
wrong words
so I've
gone on too
long. And the gulls
came back.
And the trucks outside.
I know
the loneliness
of love and
the loneliness
of being
outside
and looking
out the
window
when

love is gone. But
this face
that turns
and listens
in my
home &
wonders
if you know
me is
lost &
will never
be found. And
something
new starts
up in
my building
a different
sound.

Noggin

If I get
this little
sleep
I'm butter
pulling
the greasy
details
over everything

Harp

Once when
we were
broken up

I set up
a Christmas
tree & covered
it in pink
light. &

went out &
bought a teevee
set that
did every
thing. which

is now
a symbol
of decay

& yet I
want to
slather
my
self
in
that
day

Car Notebook

walking down the
street in
her office

he's in the middle
of cleaning

he's picking his nose

she locks her salon
tightly to protect
her from the street

it watches.

and I thought
just as my stories
are redundant
so are your
expressions

head bob
cause the toll

keeper
liked our song
I wanted to live
in that world.

this is what they
mean by traffic
can I show you my year

a branch fell and a car hit it and the leaves scattered

you got Ringo all
charged up and someone's delivering pizza
at the next exit

a dog doesn't need to go to college

the shape of this journey
is never the same each
part bloats and shrinks each
time

I'm hungry and I can't think
so my intellect is base

George Harrison changes.

Not half a tank.

Mountainous trees.

Wet Paris

a little dog
afraid of lightning
stands up to speak
hey MUTT
be brave
I felt an
empty spot
with all the
men standing
outside the
bookstore
Notre Dame
never was
so brave
and the river
have you ever
been here
before. Yes
I was when
I was a
kid
wasn't Paris

just a man
who loved
a woman
too much
that's how
the story goes
I am starving
& the traffic
is slow. I've
missed the whole
brouhaha
about concept
ualism
because
I am sleepless
& corny
isn't that
enough
must I lay
down my
heart
I brought
my chalice
up right to
the fountain
hi Alice
and I drank.

Walter Myles

Now I'm just praying that the phone doesn't ring
I'll just unplug
and leave the chocolate bar in my pocket
explaining the performance of god to Joan
as if she needs it
the silver card case slipping out of my
ass pocket the same ass that was calling somebody
as it was walking up the stairs
the city retained its luridity
tonight and all day like the floor of my apartment
retains the shit stains of Walter Myles
dog I loved for three weeks and three days
uttering his name secretly greeting
Nike in the street
hello Nike (Walter Myles) giving me his best dumb
grin
if I don't pick up shit early on in a poem
they won't think I love them
anymore when really I pee in the tub
I wanted to be carried so I took a train
thinking of Chloe wandering around under the earth
like Frank O'Hara on the beach

thinking of Akilah lying down it seems shocking
she died with Judith Butler on her mind
but we don't really know
the house I lived in is gone
the house I'm living in is always changing
I carry a tiny dog coat in my pocket
in my dream the opportunity to sing with the Beatles
was coming up inserting my band into theirs
and ours was chiefly composed of red
or redness. I propose we all jump into the water
that beach right down there and enthusiastically
I woke up. How could being just a little bit more
dogless be the source of all the rooms
changing in my house. Suggesting
we just plunge in. I knew I was off the charts by
    announcing
my dream. Two women do that and all the men
walk away. Is that what Aristophanes meant
worse than not having sex with them I start talking
about having sex with myself loving my own
mind. If heterosexuality means anything
other than me denying the existence of my own
dream I'd like to hear about that something
else and call that love. I call that war.
Years of silent repression of female dreaming
women looking like men but dreaming
they're women inside other women dreaming
that. What are men dreaming except that all women
are stupid and loving them. If you're dreaming
    something different

tell me your dreams about that. I am doomed to love
you that's for sure. Because you laugh when I say
to a man a woman is just a throne
turned upside down. A repository of his kingliness.
My kingliness does not require a throne
It is a throne. I love you because of your similar self
love and it makes me laugh. Perhaps I can have some
    chocolate
while this is going on. It will not break the spell.
I no longer live in the site of tremendous
dog fights. Certainly I could be kinder.
Black Swan was a moral film. Wouldn't you say.
I am a giant fan of Darren Aronofsky
who has the name of a dentist
and whose films are fountains of power
fountains of gender
I dreamed that Judith Butler once suggested my
    girlfriend liked my
phallus better than hers.
This is true apropos Akilah's death.
It turned out my girlfriend was much more in love with
her own phallus than anyone knew. In one film he was
    madly counting
in another he tore the refrigerator apart
jumped into blackness
jumped into white. What else do you want a movie
to do. If I had the time I'd make a film. "It gets worse"
that's what I'd call it. If he can lie so can I.
Cause there's nothing better than knowing so
much. Seeing that look in her eyes.

Bright days wandering around the block
with a dog. Breaking out. Tossing some water into a pot
    and putting in so much
cereal not knowing what the formula is. We dare it.
How long will I be boiling chicken
it's a little red inside. The dream is the perfect object
because you only can imagine its contours
you're scraping along its curves like a giant woman
lying outside. She is enormous naked and you are blind
but if you just stay with her perimeter, no her mounds
leading you higher and higher, her awesome
neck so sensitive
her ear, no ear has
ever been less constructed to hear but to allow
the midgets of myth to tickle, to bite and gnaw
if you can extrapolate some meanings from
this. Like those people who wound up going to parties
either dressed like Gertrude Stein
or Susan. She was just a big ole man
who went to Harvard.
I mean they probably burned the witches
right there before the lynching began
same tree. Stupidly at Jill's memorial I began discussing
    the publication
of her letters with Ingrid. What was I thinning.
That's right. The k is missing. Small ghostly dog
wrapped in a sheet. Eyes glimmering.
Everyone grinned when I went back to the restaurant
    and picked
my silver card case off the floor. The name is Paladin.

Never say anything bad about anyone from
HARVARD. That obsesses me. How could you say
     anything
good or is that just implied. The one more thing was
     single moms
and there was another thing. You're losing the dream
all the time. That's why we love it. I thought it was the
     dream
that was both vulgar and important. It is the search.
So he sent a letter to the addresses of each of the women
who had died. The exact address. And that was enough.
You are waiting for somebody timeless
but everything only happens inside
time. One envelope in the pile has a stamp
and you CAN find it. That she got a grant for being a
     poet
doesn't mean that she's
one and you're not. You'll get a donut too.
But what was it. Janine spoke about writing so much
     and so fast that
it wasn't writing at all. The most beautiful thing I ever
     heard.
You can see the pages in the light
every day. Notebooks full of that stuff. The blonde girl
     writing. Her passion pouring
on the page. And we can't read it. That was her dream. To
     be doing
that. Smiling years later and telling us her crime. Utterly
unreadable. No text at all, just script. Pure sex
sweat, effort, time. She said just to live here, to have all of
     you

around me now. Just the fact
that it gets cold again. It makes me hungry.
There's nothing wrong with that.
Climbing all over her naked bod. He was the man tied
    up
and they were small. And it's interesting that he also
proposed eating babies. I mean why not.
Say she raised them to kill them. I say they lived to die.
We watch them dying here, whether we go
to the ceremony or not.
That a king learned to speak
somehow is not such
a wonderful thing.
That a woman learned
to die
is.

Each Day I Get Up

for Noel Black

I think I'm kind of Morrissey
don't you
though his sweatshirt
wouldn't be so
cheap
though he'd
probably wish
that it
was. It's kind of impossible
to be famous
and not have
beautiful things
even old things.
People always give
you their best.
My mission
was to live out the fate
of anyone
anyone famous
of course
but anyone

famous
doesn't quite
land like
that. It's like
being a deity
when your
foot hits
the earth
you're someone.
I've had
the other
kind of
success.
I was at Target
with some
very cool
people. And
we all had
needs. You could
hardly get
us out of
the store. And I got
driven all
the way
back to New York
by someone who
wanted to see
Morandi's
show. It sounded

Disney
to me
but later
I saw it
with who?
Someone. And the
colors were
plain
like time. His
project was
as simple
as an old
suit, an old
Italian suit
and he was
a contemporary
of Jackson
Pollock. Famous
then against
them
like when
you got
reviewed
by somebody's
enemy &
you become
a spear.
Time has
given us

Morandi
again.
When the clatter
has stopped.
I had been
thinking Noel
you should
do something
new but maybe
not. Anyone
can see your
work has
its own
special
effect.

We Are Stardust

There was the earth
looming for the first time
in the window of the scientists
and a green ashtray
there
by his elbow
full of butts

G's Body

They all want power & the way
They'll get it through
Magic
They write in community
& we feel safe
as audience. It's weird.
I imagined
Leaning over did
You work in San Francisco
I realized she worked
Here trying to make the com
puter work. The moment between
Her legs forever she says
What is real. Transmissible form
In death or Tibetan letters
As Robert said earlier
Made of light or
Made for pouring it

BP

If I set my blackberry at "normal" what will I get
besides a paler icon on its screen
that's silent and that seems weird
who taught their students to never
say weird. I'd be speechless so much
of the time. In fact "weird" is the mitten
I keep my normal *in*
so there.
The bottom line's gotta be class
I write in this now
hardly able to remember the word
that means she writes like she sounds
I like the breath of a stretch
you read that, hear me
go *oh*
otherwise it's just all smeared out there
for you to reject

I'm a little sad
and we all agreed a room of us that it was

important to say: I'm feeling it now
are you
the tiniest rectangle of trees under bamboo
thank god gets me out of this impossible
tilt on the medium of why don't I tell him
what I'm working on now: novel
my novel's skinny
I have a movie to watch so I don't
have to do this. I can express even
less commitment
my girlfriend sends me a picture in which she
looks melancholy and I a self-hating
fool: giddy. Is it reduced to colon
it's almost like I'm grabbing
your attention by its two
tits and going: dig this.

The City

for Stephen Boyer

is juicy & bloody at night
stabbing my eyes
an orange
dog walking
through a town of dead
leaves
or the green stripe
of chicken
smell

OFF/ON

occupy invented
the city
at night
all its empty wares
are everywhere
now
now is a wide cement
path

I love when she performs
that orange stripe
madly again & again
in the house

she likes inside her cage
& she likes out

there is water every
where
when the bottom drops
out

O mammal
you are my love

my loneliness an illustrious
path a screen

I shoot these themes
themes
I mean my
jism
that look on your face
is covered
with my thought

I might stop
for a long while
now; then again I may
not

This is the big machine
and we are
in it

occupy ruined every
thing; the city
is gone
the meat trucks
cry

in this chalice
in this cherished
empty
bell

capitalism gnawing on its
bone its bloody
blazing empty
bone its porny
plastic bone

& no one's home

I scrawl on your
wall your how many mill
buildings paid
for with skulls

the girls who were stolen
& married (spent)

the boys who were
burned they are living
in your rooms
your clothes
ass
hole
are theirs

15 minutes

the beaming ~~sun~~
sun
out there
resembles
a lightbulb
the sun
is that bright
Asheville is on a mountain
of Crystal
that inspired me
I had to get out of there
fast
depending on who
uses it
anything
you make
can
be broken
reset
I can hear the faint
pattern

of the water
falling on tin
or stainless
steel. Its ugly
little message
doesn't annoy me
so much as make
me wonder
if it's making
lines in the air
my coffee is so
black and that's complete
and so I must
break it. I had
so much to say
today and yet I stretched
out. I thought "62."
That's 8. And Cathy
said today was
a full moon. It means
everything: how I turned
my hip on the slide
and almost hurt
myself. The tray that
sat in my mother's
house forever
is on my counter
now. Useless and like

forever. Greedy about
time these fifteen
minutes. It begins nailing
the sink like
a rattle has a finale.
Rather than allowing
me to search Doug
gently cut me off.
And this is enough.

The check could've been
larger. I wanted you
to be charmed by
how she lived with the plants
and the clocks
in the house. My insane
devotion to my
mother. I will not call
her. To thank her
on this day, an 8. No
I am enjoying
my rattling coffee
the sound of the knife
its drips really slicing
time which is
sound as whole
as I know. I understand
my perfect love
for you and this

is apart from that too.
Coffee like a black
pen on my birthday
a sound that is making lines
a hand that will fill
them. I deposit
my check. I say
thank you mother.

our happiness

was when the
lights were
out

the whole city
in darkness

& we drove north
to our friend's
yellow apt.
where she had
power & we
could work

later we stayed
in the darkened
apt. you sick
in bed & me
writing ambitiously
by candle light
in thin blue
books

your neighbor had
a generator &
after a while
we had a little
bit of light

I walked the
dog & you
were still
a little bit
sick

we sat on a stoop
one day in the
late afternoon
we had very little
money. Enough for
a strong cappuccino
which we shared
sitting there &
suddenly the
city was lit.

A Gift for You

around 5:30 is
a beautiful peaceful
time
you can just
hear the dog
lapping
David lifts his smoke
to his
lips forever
dangling chain
in the middle
of everything
bout the top shelf
or so. The party
at which
I sd that's my col-
lected
works and every
one
stared my home
was so small
is it

I'm not particularly
into the task
of humility
at the moment
but I'm
not against
it
it's like that
deflated
beach ball
on a tiny
chair

I think of as
joking
with the larger
one on a
painting
floating in air
my home
is large
love made it
large once
not to
get all
John Wieners
& believe
me love made
it small

once
this place
only had
sex unlike
the house
I love a house
I fear a house
a house never
gets laid
frankly who
doesn't like
a hotel
room
I live in a
hotel
room a personal
one. A young
person very
much like me
was brutal
no personal
photographs
please   it was
anyone's
home perfect
for a party
now I'm
going fast. How
the description

of a drug
enters
a room
& changes
the room
thus
with going
fast
say thus
if you
want to go
slow. To drink
the wrong
thing for a
moment
for you
to lick my
thigh
& your
honey
face

I met a dog
named
Izzie
once, I
met a
dog named Alan
the calm

person writing
her calm
poems
now & then
she shows
her sacred
heart
she opens
her chest &
a monkey
god
is taking
a shit
swinging
on his
thing. You didn't
know I
had so
much inside
me buckets
of malice
bibles
of peace
I don't want
to go
all library
on you
now like
my mother

the mother of
god or
my brother
named
Jack who
sat in
a deck
of cards
getting
hard
when she squeezes
in getting
cozy I know
less what
I want
to say. I can open
an entire

room comes
out each
moment that's
what I mean
not things
widen &
flow there's
no purpose
to this.

The Baby

The baby
says to the old
man let's
have a cup
of coffee
the old
man says now
you're talking

St. Joseph Father of Whales

St. Joseph
father of whales
speak to us
from the deep
St. Joseph
Baby father traveler
clown suit
not father
but carter
of watermelons
and cantaloupes
and footballs &
my fearful
agony; carter
of my coyote
　　joy
carter of pearly
landscapes
your tattooed
soul is a teevee
　　set
across which gallop

kangaroos and jave
          linas, dancing
cigarettes, grief
and me with a staff
leading a legion
of puppies
out of the desert
with your picture
on my staff
but it's you as a dog
in a baseball
cap. I heard your
Joseph Josephy
songs in the whales
          last night
giant round giggly organs
tickling and mooing
and diving calves, you're
the oldest & the silliest
Joe—need to keep
you on my
side. Thanks to you
I'm enormous and slippery
thanks to you I'm
sleek. I break
the bank breachy breachy in my thoughtful
wishes for the world
and wolves and growly leaves
dancing behind holy

rice shades, thanks
to you Joe
I can read the
leaves and the
sky & sing along
with them
in the end
I have you to thank
for my transparency
here I am gentle
thumping heart & lungs
at the bottom of
the ocean; here
I am your visible whale
sun keep watch
on my blubber
sailing around and
past that man
eyes me gently
thanks Joe
of the desert
Joe of the sky &
of outer space
gleaming pluto &
mars big
Jupiter
& the sea the surveying
man feels my
reasonable guts &

the gleaming chart
of all my trips
& the goodness
ahead & he smiles
with an infant's
trust

Dream

Close to the
door in
my dream the
small signs

I saw a brown
sign with wisdom
on it
I saw a brown
one leaning
with wisdom
on it

fringe of a mirror
my mother
leaning over a pond
cupping water

leaning against
the moulding
cardboard or
wood which materials do you

does your wisdom prefer

which a-
partment in a summer
with someone
I felt brave to
have touched
her love the screen
door and the dogs
and the cats always
getting out. That
was the fear
two signs
fading but recalling
they had faded like words
fade in stone because
of the rain and the days
and waking and the dream
is leaving with every
step leaning over the meat
because I do not want
you to have died in vain
kissing the turkey and
the neck of my dog
all animals am I.
all dreams, all stone
all message am I.

Dream 2

the car had a cover over it
and it was over the wheels
and it hurt my ass and I
couldn't sleep. It seems I should move, go forward now
I was wandering through the jungle
anywhere on earth but I was a woman
in bed in New York and how many
people have died in wild places
dreaming you were still in bed
would you know. Travel well
I said to my dog when she
went on her journey thinking
of a cheap movie
I've thought this was an urn
turning this was on water
this was flat
but now I see light between
the trees I see water trickling
through stone this is not
made of language but energy
that will stop when I die
the dream dies too
one bolt

for you

the shape
of this

& her smell

& the shine in the small
lit room
to the boy

replace him
w you &
let me love
that shine
in you

let me.

After the Season

You can find all the clothes you
didn't want on ebay
I wish something would come & clean
My bookshelves
I'm just going to write a few minutes
I'm just going to write an hour
I imagined the dogs watching teevee
for centuries all those different clothes
doors opening and closing
why do I want those books
I want other books
nothing turning into moons
the loose seat held down
by an ass
the restaurant felt like winter to me
and the waitress said isn't it great
it feels like spring
the toilet bursting with joy
hallucinatory elvis
shriveled into a mild lesbian
committed to living narrower
& more fully

till she's seated in a humble
cave
I can't erase anything here
or change anything
I just want to write a few years
everyone felt if they stayed in southern
C-A-
well eventually I would just climb
into the library and be a book
I'd be preserved
and you'd come around and live
in my home and my dog would be born again
in your eyes; in those mountains and hills

Sept 18

A great deal
was lost
by writing
you know. Writing
was deplored
& led to the loss
of memory.
I am building
a big
fire.
And my legs
are burning
from the
electrical
one

this pas-
time
of leaning
one up
on the other
is strange-

ly in–
cendiary.

If
I have
a good
talk
it stops.

We bray
our
love. He
doesn't
ring
my bell
either
we chime. Dave
pointed
out the don–
key
in the field.
Alone
with
the sheep

and Ire–
land. Country
with
a donkey

in
it. Two
women
on the
phone
No more se-
cret
messages
for you
No more
you. Just
this open
field. He
Haw.

Washington

why does he get
a whole state
all the way
over here
it took
me a long time
to figure out
that she
was mary shelley
not the whore of
god. All that
desire
my cell phone
dinks like quotes
carrying
you, a sign
leaning against
a car & my ass
clenches
in the sun for
you. And I see a cloudy
mountain

of trees. It's you I adore.
Dink. It's you I'm
breaking my back for.
I play rolling the dog
with a hairless
woman. A car tucked
in a gully. The ins & outs
of EMBODY ROAD.
The light so truthful
about your embodiment
and I swear off
complaint
not bliss. Without
a punchline
without a fart
grapes scatter &
kill our son while
baby sneakers
dangle in
my view. Am I responsible
for this. I will
kiss you tattoo. Zing.
Every kind of sound
is your love.
I'm copying us to the road.
When I draw those scratching
peaks I won't
be waiting. He's here.
the soft pencil sound

scratching our length &
time. Erasing, blurring
and blowing. We're marking
forever. Get this.

I am recording you.
I will keep you in my gut.
the cars are stalled.
Zounds the trucks. Litter and
it will hurt.
report violators.
Dog where? or is it dogware.
Is it the drifting mfa
the new. Bearded man
and his beauty. Us. The collective
beast. A box forces
its way through the tossled
angles of tree points.
Dink. And now the river
wrinkly cuss. Ka thunk
ka thunk

what about YOUR blathering genitals
that's an aside.

I would like to do something
before we mourn
the end of American
democracy. At least to

dive into a joint
and explode something
(I feel fear)
to become conscious
And one.
To be seen. All stars
at once. As
gleaming people
I know myself, pushing.

To My Flowers

Why
did you just
come and
die.

El Diablito

I let you wisp in here a little
There that's nice
lights flashing
music thumping
I'm heading to do a reading
of course
the cute waitress delivers the guys'
food & I'm afraid she caught
me making eating faces
seriously now saying
goodbye to Thich Nhat
Hahn how many people always
think about you when they are
chewing. There's hardly anything on
the planet that isn't improved
by a little lime; happy squeeze
this sailor will never get scurvy

I wonder if she feels different
when she serves him
Today at the gym this woman
said you always look so cute

one of the few times I ever
looked at my x's twitter
feed someone had told her
she had beautiful hair
I thought gross what a narcissist
Well it's not like I said someone
at the gym said I ALWAYS
look cute on social media
No one may ever read this
maybe some archivist at Yale
will wind up with my phone
and lean over to another
graduate student look someone
at the gym told her she ALWAYS
looked cute. Covers his mouth
laughing. Maybe I'll lose this
phone. Narcissistic little thought
You will not die alone
I'll read you tonight
at KGB.

Angel

I suppose
I'm afraid
of forever
I close
my eyes
& it's intense
it's beginning
inside me
I'm trying
to clear the deck
to get to
this
yawning simplicity
it's something
different
in the dark
how many times
could I
move the dot
back to
hear him say
there was

so much
more of it
& there is
will you love
me forever
for this
my simple
fear
my fear of the
dark gives
me something
to say
it descends

I wake
each glimpse
like a tiny
star of
the other
side
when I
was alive

Sharing Fall

I lost
my loss
in a collective
of loss
I could reach
in and grab
a fist of
them saving
them from
the rain
my mouth is
red for every
child who
has starved
eating
the corpse
of their
father or
mother. My corpse
is spaghetti
sharing birthdays
w a famous

clown
a famous
blind man
& a famous
actor. This cool
makes me
want to
divulge
go on exposing
my hunger
which is
the only
story I
know Tin
bliss
filling this
air and
every air
my only
love a watch
and a dead
one to be sure
renewed by
an ugly face &
what I love
in a box
shoved up
on a shelf
& I wonder

when I'll
take her
down &
abuse
her again
or disabuse
her of
her stupid
notions
about her
self. Silly
little filly
racing
around &
around.
My dog hates
my farts
should
I fart
here. If the
place is
too gross
I tell my
neighbor
not to call
me mommy
& he's not
my neigh
bor

anymore
I only work
in his
world so
I sit with dogs
so it's
clear
when we
wag our tails
we do not
work at
all. I've
only been
getting to know
you better
my rasquach
ismo
is mo
only way

I'm pulling back
from that
border
I let the yellow
handles
of your genius
your sunny front
against
all insult

your sunny
golden leaves
half
a can
I can't remember
what I said
this is a translation
of weather
how is it in Baltimore
Today
I couldn't
even get
there without removing
another city
the device warned
me don't remove
all of them
I removed
all of them
and all these cities
are gone

Paradise

which
I never know
how to
spell it's
with me always

Notell

It seems an unimaginable
Forest
I'm not talking to my
self I'm conducting
an extremely in
timate exchange with my
government
My brash smile
Means it's okay
Someone's dancing in
Clogs. It sounds
That way suctiony
I'm not here to con
Fuse the government
What I've
Got I share. The rubied surface of
Deteriorating cities moves me
That *is* what we're doing
Everyone getting
Off here

I feel like being smart
As soon I seem stupid
I top it all up
I put on my cap.
There are machines all
Over the place. My friend
sat behind
The queen. Perfectly lucid
but Elizabeth
Kept going wtf she wouldn't
Shut up. Philip & Charles
Kept going
Mother.

beautiful cows

covering

the hill

more cows

I'd kind

of like

to buy

a cow

and that makes

me want

to cry

The City of New York

Tom Otterness is dead
now his tiny little statues
are filling the corners
of the New York subway
like dirty chess pieces.
Why has his death
made their annoying
        presence

mausoleum out of our
cranky lumbering
cars
our glinting caskets
a lot of people
are dead you know
I'm in the years
when it's not yet most
instead I sing of this
thing I'm on
& Tom
I might talk to his
wife: habits

details occurring in the time
of this commission
how did he get it.
His last. It makes me strong.
We're all friends our boots
sway on the el
the beauty of our angles
illumination
our beigeness in the rain
for a moment I was unperturbed
with Myra
her tone when she greets
me—I am quasi late
I sink into the tyranny
of my business
Shoving it into hers
& Chana's. The two of
them glowering & bickering
before the drive to the country
& next week to france.
Is Dia entirely staffed by
females
Lauren was, Barbara is
Brighde was. Only Charlie
& he's gone & a
new guy coming in.
What happened to Lynn.
Do I know her. Sort of.
Kind of. Never did.

In the evening the voice
on the train was warning
us about thieves &
sexual perverts
this woman & I
started snuffling
the voice began again.
What's next we laughed.
He said thanks. The younger
woman was decidedly
cruising. The subway is hot.
I'm thinking this.

what *was* my thought
rain in my eye
what did I say
the city being the only place
that corresponds to my
need
to be every place
at once

Paint Me a Penis

If the best thing the world discovered today is that at
    the inside
of the universe is a cat
I love your braids; I love your peaceful eating
I hate that the sum total effect of the schedule
was sadness. Did you read the schedule. Nope.
I'm jealous. If he used the same words
over and over again in plays and movies and commencement
addresses is that wrong. Is art wrong. What if art is wrong.
Is there only one sun. Some planets have two.
When the rain was pouring I wanted to be in here
silent with you. In the dog's beady black gaze. In the room
with the sleeping dog. With you leaving the room.
I've stopped the rain, I've silenced you.
I think the story was that one woman had gotten
the painting from the other when they were dating
but she never paid for it and then she moved out.
The painting sat in the second floor window and the painter
saw it and demanded it back. No. So the painter wrote
Marie O'Shea give me back my painting and put
it in the window opposite. She's a mess. We call her
twat. When it blasted I asked you to put

your headphones on. The dog's wheezing. I think
smack in the middle of that time was a virus
and it gave itself to everyone freely. We learned that
everything was related to everything else. Just as everything
was getting more separate and no longer a simple bowl
of fruit everyone was dying of the same thing. Not everyone.
Later when they hit the buildings it was just like everyone
in the city felt it. Not the same. We felt the shake. The
    request
in the air was how do we all feel it now. It wasn't the same.
It was like you kept breaking off another square of the
bar and tasting it. He came running back into the room.
He was *moaning*. And now he just stares. And the rain
starts up again. I've never been invited to one mooting.
Do they have them. I remember the time I was invited
and we went around the room saying how we came
to be there. I was invited and everyone
stared and they never let me know when they were
meeting again. She wore a yellow dress. Everyone's
    watching you. He stands
in the doorway watching you eat. It stopped.
I want the painting in the window. Yeah. And you can
really ask her questions when you get her alone. And you
    were reading all the
time. And you said it a lot, that you wanted one which
you don't remember. I guess I wanted one. Now some
people in that mysterious time there it goes again
decided to in a very dedicated way begin talking about it
because there wasn't enough of that. That part had waned.
    Otherwise

you could just take it off the walls, you could go to funerals
and get fucked. You could recite it so that all they saw
was you. Huge numbers of them banded together marching
slowly into the room. There's footage of us dancing. I
   wouldn't ask
the stars to be quiet but I'm closer to them now. She was so
smart. I'm serious. I bet she'd make a good one. Since I
   didn't grow
my own I'd like to see what she'd make me. If he demands
   that no
one tells theirs at the breakfast table I think he probably
   pulls
it out of his pajamas and slaps it on the table. Dreams to
   me are
always receding. It's the only perfection: it's vanishing,
   stoking my
appetite so I'm drawing it for you as it becomes less the
   experience
that just happens as I'm resurrecting it for you. I'm making
   it
for you. I'm asking her. Make it for me. I'd like that. I'm
   putting it
in real deep. Out there, where everyone is.

Large Large
White Flowers

for Susie Timmons

I'm using this
it's large
but it could leave it could
change
inside of changing
is hanging
everyone crossing the street
was talking to some
one; alone
to be w people
sending off
their rays
I'm sticking w you
even less
nuanced. Less smell
maybe
a blue pigeon
unlocks the
door to Susie
to the slabs

of wood
on Delancey
white planks &
then really beautiful
planks of artificial
wood leaning
against a tree
why is this pithy
to me. I'm re
lieved to be living
one day
without camera
or pen or
watch
I felt totally un
watched
alone w this
non assignment
this deliberation
to be glad
for New York
that contains
dogs & statements
experimental
art; art of yore
and that blue
pigeon that
followed the wood

but has
a pigeon ever been blue
before or the
night in such
stripes
go out
without your phone
call no one
Honey's hunching on
the rug
the intactness of
all experience
descrves our wavering
but eventual
respect. Call mc after
everything
I have some
love. Rather
than apologizing
I'm doing
well
rather than letting
you go
I'm letting you
leave
blue pigeon
I've got your
back

and the vista
that surrounds

you is magnificent
I'm leaving
it there!

Dissolution

sometimes I forget what country I'm in
I could write poems in bed
I think
have some Americans
look at your awful mov-
ie to tell you when
you're wrong
& just racist. I got this bug bite
     that could be anything.
Got no new information
to send across. I'm willing
to embrace new sorta cray-
ony tone
     scribbled version
of empty so it's kind
of full. A kid could draw this world
it
had been lived in
so long.

You forgot

to call your family
& now you're ready to write an
explicit
bible of love.

The ripple
of experience is the
only beauty here.

My coloring book
why not is so
like a movie. And I just hand you this damp
coloring book
I say there. That's my model.
Not the kind of laminate
shit you can bring
in the tub. I'm not making some
picture book of bourgeois
life. A damp
coloring book
is naturally
orange. You left
it outside   *now* you want to save
it?   It's still good
          and that's your secret.

How did a mosquito
get under these sheets. Knocking
against my calf. They
stop when I stop
thinking about them. The book
that was my very
private thing
is gone.

August 23

eternity of yard
sales
then I pass
a road named
Old Revolutions

estate sale
to think

& I pull out

orange diamond
advising me

embroidery

cock a doodle
doo
oh c'mon

I want to
get a house
inna dog
inna not rifle
take hormones
for myself
grow mountain
beard

u click to know me
Truck

turkeys pass

woods foam
when it rains

Tom & *now* it's beeping
again. Can you
fix it. still beeping

on wednesday I can

& no one tell the
mountain

Crows again.

count shirts & shorts &

the dark
clouds
coming in. Will I al-
ways confuse

a moment in my life
for the rest of my life

when truly
it was
fun

Photograph of everything

you three
kids in
the water
burying the rock
splash in pink
& purple
the mountain
of trees &
the cloud
just above
I look at my
knees

I'd
like a
nice mom
who lived
in the
country
I could
visit once
in a

while
kids
need reg
ularity
so that
won't
work. O
sun. Stay
here.

Sylvia

Later the whole
generosity
of dogs & the
silver
sun. My loneliness
like a sash
that boat
in the distance.
Triangle
heart. Sylph
w a beard
got wet &
gleam-
ing black.

What I like
about you.

go deeper
now
into the
present

out there
with
the kid
on the swing
everybody
sit there.
Doesn't
mean I'll be here
when I am.

Kids out there.
What is divinity.
Turns out something
really large
is on the
swing.

Acceptance Speech

First I want to say this feels incredible. To be female, to run and run and run to not see any end in sight but maybe have a feeling that there's really no outside to this endeavor this beautiful thing. You know we don't have a single female on any of our bills. And what about two women, two women loving. Or even more. A lot of women. A lot of money. Is there a message that I failed to receive that the face of woman cannot be on our money. And what about that house I just won that white one. When I sit there and if I sit there and I've got to tell you I'm not sure I want to sit there. Some of you might remember my first campaign yes that was back in 1992. Few men have run for twenty-four years. Twenty five by the time I stand and take the oath in January to serve my country. I did not quit I stand here with you on this beautiful rapturous day sunny day in New York to turn around, to look back and look at all that we've won. But I'm getting ahead of myself. Let's get back to that house. That white house. We often hear these words even as an explanation of what metonym means. Are you familiar with this term. yes I promise you poetic presidency. The white house speaks is a metonym. Certainly that white house we speak of is not the whole government. Like Fred Moten says it is incomplete. But it has come to be a symbol of it. And I think two things. I think whiteness, I think of the whiteness of the house and I think of house-ness. It houses the government. Now that I have won it offers to house me now. I now officially make that white house a homeless shelter. It is a complete total disgrace that we have people without homes living on the streets of America. I have lived with them. Not for long periods of time but in the same way that I am the first president who knows what women feel because I am a woman, I am one, I have also eaten chicken with the homeless. I ate at the Bowery mission. Very rubbery, very chewy chicken. Those chicken were not happy when they lived and they are no happier being chewed on dead at the Bowery mission, and the chewers are not happy either, no. So here's the future good food at the white house for all the homeless in America. You know who the homeless are. They are military men and women. Who fought our pointless wars, who came home after each stupid greedy war we have waged and they got less. Is there a GI bill for veterans of Iraq and Afghanistan. I'm not sure but I don't think so. Can they buy a house. Who can buy a house. Under Myles they have bought the white house. That is my gift. The white house will house the mentally ill, out patiented during the great president Reagan, meaning he threw them out of the house, the mentally ill, thrown out of the American house, and the alcoholics who do not have free and abundant and available treatment? Cause this country breaks our hearts. We will habit them too. We will occupy all government buildings and memorials housing and holding and loving the homeless and the sick and the starving. We'll do what the statue says. you know liberty. We will take buildings and we will build buildings and our culture our new America will begin to live. Our government needs to be in the business of living not dying, what else is a government for. The government will become more departmental and take you in, you and your wonderful needs. We'll start with the Department of Women. Obviously to say women matter and do matter so much and a lot we need a distinct place in the government to specifically focus on female concerns which is parity mainly, reforming congress so that if America is increasingly diverse in a multitude of ways our congress must represent those groups percentage wise that's smart don't you think. So if most of the people in America are female so should be our government right. America is not a department store. We want to do more in our country than shop online and at the mall. Let's face it everyone is home shopping and yelling at each other at their computers. The malls are falling apart. The malls are pretty much gone. Let them go. We want to make real departments for who we really are. Not shopping. We will be stalwart, we will be strong. Let's go. Let's go out. We are out there now. We are here on the highline. Yes.

That's the way it works under Myles. Early on I described a department of culture. We will have that. We will have art in America, not just the magazine, just for starters we will multiply the budget of the NEA by tenfold. We will bring back CETA, that was like an art workers program we had in the eighties but we will call it SEE THE . . . SEE THE . . . what I don't know. I just got elected, I haven't worked everything out but just think of the possibilities. SEE THE sky, SEE THE river over there, SEE THE Whitney, a lot of people will be walking around appreciating and we will pay them. There will also be the HEAR THE program, the SMELL THE program. That's probably what you're going to do early on with all those you know recovering veterans who don't have to live on the streets. Get them in on the SEE THE, SMELL THE, HEAR THE programs. We're going to massively fund libraries, open twenty four hours, and they will not be filled with homeless people because they will have homes, so the libraries will be filled with people reading and watching movies, and going into the conversation rooms and having conversations and so on. All education will be free, trains will be free. Cars will eventually be banned. Cars are stupid. No more pumping oil, no more fracking. Everything will be driven by the sun, or else be plugged in electrically. Electric something. There'll be lots of free food. A lot of archery. Everyone will be a really good shot. We'll get good at aiming, intentions, not killing. Oh yeah and we'll send a lot of masseuses to Israel and Palestine.

Everyone needs a good rub. No more pesticides, here, anywhere, lots of small farmers, an amazing number of stand up comedians, and lots of rehearsal spaces and available musical instruments and learning centers for people like myself who would like to play something, perhaps a guitar. Nobody would be unemployed. Everyone would be learning Spanish, or going to the sex center for a while having ejaculation contests, or just looking at porn for a while and going out into the yard and helping the farmers improve the crops. Just gardening. Helping the flowers. Distributing the flowers. SEE THE flowers. When in doubt always just being a SEE THE person for a while. There'll be a whole lot of people encouraging people to SEE THE. We want the SEE THE to thoroughly come back. There'd be an increase in public computers, like water, like air, have we stopped the oil and the fracking early enough to protect the water and air, we hope so but there will be a decrease in private computers with an enhanced desire to be here, exactly here where we are, which some would argue is *there* on the computer which of course would be allowed but being *here* would be cool, some people meditating, other people just walking around, smiling feeling good about themselves, living shamelessly and glad. Guns would be buried. Guns would be in museums and people would increasingly not want to go there. Gun museums would die. What was that all about. Money would become rare. I would have a radio show as your president and also I might be on television and also I just might want to talk to you. In the tradition of American Presidents like Fiorello LaGuardia the little Flower I would be president Edward Myles, the woman, changing my name, very often, would probably be good I would like that and I would write a new poem for you each week. I might just walk around saying it and eventually you would forget I was the president. I would go to the gym. There are people who like to manage things just like there are people who like to play cards and the managers would change often enough and they would keep the parks clean,

America increasingly turning into one big park, one big festival of existence with unmarked toilets and nightly daily events and free surfing lessons and free boards, just put it back when you're done and a good bed for everyone, I just slept in the best bed last night and I slept on the plane sleep is great nobody would be short of sleep everyone would be well slept, chaotic and loving hearted and have all the time in the world to not kill, to love and be president everyone take your turn and dance. Dance now. I love my fellow citizens. It is good to win. Thank you. I feel like I had a bad dream last night that like the head of the FBI decided to steal the election by making shit up about me because I am female but that wasn't true and we are really here undeluded, un mucked up. Wide awake in America for once. See the see the see all of your fabulous beauty and your power and your hope. Thanks for your vote. And I love you so much thanks.

Western Poem

purple clouds
my doubts

iridescent
cream, my
loss

purple mountains
my friends

buzzards circling
overhead
my hopes

birds singing
jagged singing
my indecision

wrecked skinny
tree
my past

photographs
I send home
my indiscretion

amber
street
light
my reading

my appetite
my appetite

red striped sky
my confusion

bright yellow
grey sky
my ardor

car lights
my commo
    tion

telephone
pole
my wishes

stop sign
my fear

family dollar
family dollar

court house
my opinion

black cloud
white sky
hesitation

black cloud
white sky
bliss

blinking signals
my intentions

black mountains
too many
suggestions

skipping white
lines
my attention

a young cowboy
first saw
the lights

a young cowboy
first saw the
lights

the horns
on your van
my defensive
     ness

that ole train
my dreams

that ole train

The Earth

It's our poem.

Jiggly

I keep
trying to get
it right
all night.
If you're
going the
wrong way
you're
responsible
for every
body. Every
living thing.

OK!

May 8

Where was I
when I'm
so happy
now
a teeny window
& in it teenier
squares
all that sitting
still in the
squalid
night & something
turning
I'm home
what if you had
to copy out
everything
you ever
wrote before
but seriously
where was
I? The other
coast of

course
not in
the tinier
squares
but one
in the same
my misconception
perhaps
standing in
for the rest
& something's
turning. I love each
whistle here
each jangling
horn. Quack &
a gush
you know the sediment
I meant
but a sediment
of sound
consider the
wind &
the brutal
horns
of night
I was in the hilly
city out
there & a puffi
ness came

over me
nudity's
back & I
hope to
find lovers
everywhere
but in
books. The revolution
remains
fleshly
washing up to
my ears & then blowing
softly
thousands of
cars the city
a tube
our nation
a scream

Epic for You

In the book
called
bed it
says
eating you
endlessly
& the
flower
turns

in bed
it says
the man
hates
his
female insides
she's
the sauce
of the world

in bed
it says

you'll
forget
time
in the
tiny room
you'll
explode
in your
knee
socks
exploding
putrid
truth
that's right
it stinks

in bed
it says
everything's
worth it
we do
it slow
what's
cool about
us is
we take
our time
not
yours

when the
clam
shut she
couldn't
work
in the
dark she
thought
about
the open
thighs
welcoming
the on
slaught

summer's
fist
cold
slap aching
mountain
collapse
ramshackle
blood

earflaps
yummy
live wire
puss

in bed he thought
I feel like
a hungry sal
amander
cartoon
wiggling
over my
girl. I slop and
shake her
thing. I shoulder
hot
cock on
parade
fucking spring &
a sex
feels
like
playdough

sort of a responsible
citizen
in bed
pound you
been dying
to eat
this orange
all day
drop its
juice

on the floor
suck up
its sections
bit. Sting
my lips
sticky
hands. What's
corny
no it's
an orange
a fucking
tasty
juicy lovely
fucking
orange
I open
my day
mouth
to you.

In bed
I said
why did I ever
think
that
I liked kids.
A woman
is just
so truthful.

May 26

I keep
to tiny
gestures
sweet
William
dazzling orange
sky. My my
my my dying
new york.

You

I'm bravely
eating my croissant
at everyone
I'm living
on my wet
board
I'm living
on my money
limits set
& the lights
lower. I worship
the blue
marks
on the hydrant
how like
the name
of a flower

You

after all these years
you should know
my font
you should know
the numbers
go in the middle
what I say

there's so many of
you why don't
you talk
each time
I have to click
and press
what's the use
of being
famous

Circus

Jill tells me about the
show she is making
& I thought it's like
Flowers. What kind
of flowers am I making.
I think that I met
you at work. I'm home
now & think what
kind of flower am
I making. How do we find
the flower, use the
flower spread it around
I thought summer's a good
Growing season or is
it. Is summer just hot?
I could bring my flowers
to your flowers, always
afraid when I show
that maybe I am making
a funeral. Whatever I am
when I show it around.
I love your flowers

a finger tip has so many
hands & you love
mine. How is it to love
for once and to see it all
now to be so afraid of loving
and dying. Mounds of
Flowers go to my head.
I love you inside there
also out, to show, I want to
bring you so many flowers.

So

I remember
standing
in San Diego
making you
film me
holding
those flowers
I was standing
still

Fuck time
I'm getting
it off
my bo
dy

in my
need
for celebration

the stewardess
almost

does dirty
talk
w the man
turkey lurkey
baby
I swear
about his
drink
bitch
it's father's
day & I'm
daddy
now & I
lift her
legs &
kiss
her asshole:
you. I hold
you in
the next
cartoon

blasted windows
of love
bangling
tits the alternation
of pain &
the gentleness
is what

I'm really
into. I meant
to tell you
this.

It's a bible
of knowing &
unknowing
I'm choosing
to live
in w you
cheroo cheroo
the sound
of our
walk

walking to
the bathroom
on the
plane I'm
unable to
text you
something
dirty making
you pop
out of
a meeting
somewhere into
a small tiny

darkened
gigantic room
smelling
of puss

puss somewhere
in the airport
ass
in the
van. Tits
pushing against the
glass of
everything
selling
everywhere
Nothing's
for sale.
I want
blood &
the rest

Time
to talk
& fork. I watch
America
mountains
pass. Watching
marking all
the time

loudmouth
in front
of me
on the plane
A woman
laughs. Ha ha
shutup
she gallops
for the
man. Silly
horse. He's high
she laughs
he laughs w
glee. shut
up

Anything I say
is not
true, forgetting
everything & the present
popping
up like memory.

Hey
look at
the mountain
tops
popping
below. Look

everything's popping
through the veil
of darkness
the range
of one state
to another
an approaching
making vision
a seat
blast in the sky
between
your legs
the crack of
an excellent
line in my
book

I sort of
think I
lost all my earthly poems
cause
I am
supposed
to do
something else.
Lives are slower
or gorgeous &
I'm growing
something
else

a ripple
of mountains
like a highly
aroused
cunt

Today

I would love to love someone
forever & fuck them till they
died.

Memorial Day

They came
back from
the army
they don't
share &
then they
get a
new phone

Today Egyptian

walking
straightforward
deep navels
broken hips
wide wingspan
smashed nose
wolf
kingly triangular
hat
black woman
black man one step
clear flasks
and tiny vials like I bought
is it a butt plug
honey I bought for you
barfing lion
jewels
clear bottle over head
one leg lifted
bow short across
seemless breast
each arrangement

I must
disheveled proxy
hole balls
modos gniegos sir
I hate money
a face mask composed
of tiny swirls
hearts on fabric
o molded faience
in time some birds are gone
and some birds and
some woman is a
blue beast
claws practically language
prong I didn't get to
copy now
I get to touch you & be
your friend to kiss
entire collection bumps
and holes
over there
sweet water; cool tools
for bird is a golden
arrow giddyup heart
fuck clueless blue elegant
holes web over web
condemned little screw
balls dark horse packed
lightly inking heart

circulating blue not
now I can't read that
and that's a later reply
in the center everything
fades flower wash
open white bowl turn
I'd give everything
for Persia
dark mussed
pardon I stumbled
on my favorite blue
rug
secula
safavida
felpa da la
sickle lives not vase
gleam and stings
away underglaze
no words
star tile
inventory of rugs &
shirts
two fools on a boat
I notice that
the flower in the flower
I think you're the
real thing; blue
flower in flower
white flower in flower

or at your center & not
oh smoke some pot
& I'll just read you
poetry
I like ya two buds
blue antelope
I want to do
everything to you
3-holed no four holed
golden spout
red wreaths round & wakes
things up
and a vase in a vase
hungry tendril reaching
cornflower surrounding

clear but dirty
clear but time
clear but golden
clear but spoken
clear but filled in
clear but branched
clear but forced
clear but occupied
clear but fled

you are not my
compass o shadow
tree that surpasses

every one
slopping yellow
teeny dark cartoon
at the heart
chip

sealed
spotted
deepened
seen
enhanced
worn
bared
promenade
'n festooned

there's pineapple outer
leafy open eye drawing
riches to me
I been to Iznik
I placed u in the wall
I sucked your leaf
into my cyclone
late invoked nipple
you pretend to be
a little more withholding
than I do
& robot rug
greasy shiny knowing

you root pushing up
day lips, berries,
hoist the juicy
flow of hands, snakes
& tears, cunty flame
through your warm love
here in my berry
tree my stadium
under my sea, w my beads
in my tall throwing pots
somebody change the kangaroos'
diaper, oh you like
the chimera, the ocelot
a lot, watch the phoenix
be burnt to a crisp
rabbits and peacocks
please be peaceful
holy & still
divide into groups
the back of a thought
is the same
you see this thing
come into view
shake deep
blurred brain
brightly shined
flower
rambling road
simply daisy

on silk, snowflake,
militarized each or
gan unique
witnessing my intention
to take something out
to dinner brite
in Iznik
dying the elephants
cry stein green
sway vulva parting clouds
or cars two nations
under one square roof
one errant blue bowl
screaming wealth
butterflies
live in the park,
a pair of Fo dogs

After Thought

I guess
what
i like
is my thousand
of little
titles
wiggling
for years.

Lark

Anything
could possibly
become any
thing else. It
was the condition
of this
dream
things could
blow themselves
right into
other things.
Not like
a collision
but a blend
it was like
there was
a wind
in this
universe
and conversion
was the rule.
I was telling

her about
the thing
ending and I
did notice
that who I
was talking
to was
my ex. Not the 2015
ex but the
2013 one. She
didn't seem
to know
who she was
or be particularly
perturbed not
to be herself
anymore. She
was simply
her. Thought-
ful. Even
a little
concerned. I
guess it
got weird
when I
tried to
talk about
my feelings.
Feelings

she shrieked
she became
the most
magnificent
storm not
even a being
anymore
but a spell
a giant
boat rocking
roar. I guess it was
pretty absurd
of me when
you put it
like that. Eileen
called the
voice out
the window. She
had come w
her husband
to pick up
the strap. Who
would want
to spend the
rest of
their life
with a fat
bearded
man but of course

that could
be Brenda
herself. I could
be this
house or that
silvery ceiling
lamp looking
down my love
that distant
car turning
passing. Tiny limbs
in the blue
sky, planes
over head
my fingers
on this pen
being everyone

sighing,
turned.

A

A person
out side
butting
up inside
at home
out side
one. Ringing
the streets
the elaborate
lighting
and the peculiar
blocks
of the neighbors
their houses
and lamps.
Pick a letter
any letter
it seems
it is broken
hearted
dripping
angel giving

it all
a squeeze
what's
got a
lot
tomorrow
a curt
ain
a home
less
ness
hold it all
French P
porpoise
Orange
the letters re-
arrange
them
selves
it's impossible
to make
a plan
any
body
auto body
all on
your
own make
a P

it was in
credible
one dog
my incredible
loneliness
I want
to roll
my genitals
in towards
a large
empty field
in which
I can say
everyone
& feel
love. The dog sprayed
my dog not
hit her
quite   I
think she
squatted
forced
out her
own rain
terrific
performance
I got
a lot. By
the time

I send
you: my
    friends

I don't
know any
one having
sex with strangers
all of
you.   Tell

me. I'm
weird
in my
moment
he ex
plained
oh these
are just
two mo
ments
important
I was
in high
school
too. Which
mouth
to kiss.
In

celebration
she is
going on a diet
then
she may
get old

I understand
you I
understand
everyone
Shannon the singers
were down
by the
lake & you pulled
the sword
from the water
it
was offered
by a

hand. In the palm
of the hand
was the letter
A

down the throat
of the singer
I wonder

what will
happen
tomorrow
every
day I get
on a plane. I miss
every

one

meet

you

in let

tered

cities

this morning

I stood
crying

I think it was after
I went
running

I said
if you
can guarantee
me
I get
as much
as the
men

I'm stuck
on your

letter

the dog's
limbs
crossed
people
liked that
my belly
a soft cushion
I went running
this
morning
straight on his
ranch
it's very
relaxing

to have one of
these legal
pads
we went to that
show
too

why would I
if you
felt that
way
if there
was a
house next year
but I
never
knew when
to come. I was
sort of ex
cited
about
you

OK I want to be
somebody's
family
but I'm
not

have your last night
of being
beautiful
or whatever
the fuck
you're
doing
with the world

I'm just
going to be a little
baby & float
off on
my tether
in out
of space

I wish
I could talk
to someone
I could
cry

terrible

It is
a little
portrait
of time dripping

wait
I've got
it on my
phone
I don't have
the sustenance
the food
to be
too happy
too long
it's just
a made
up thing
I just
want to go
wandering
off into the woods
like a dog

I'm holding
a bunch
of grapes
like a baby
I'm like
a big
slow ad
for the
failure
of love

It's almost
too sad
to walk
my dog

her bulletin
board
has a six
pack of
white
notes I can't
stop
you from urinat
ing
it's your
vital right
a dog has
a yard
it's the world
I will take
you out there

Nobody
can take care of me
I can take
care of
everyone
look at my

feet
the toes
clutching
somebody's
sheet
I am a statue
in my
way

I'm sick of
not
belonging
babe

Can anyone eat
a whole bag
of grapes
out of
sorrow

I can't hear
you

I took the dog
out to walk
and she
stood

I sd
okay & took
her in

she doesn't know
what she
wants in
a strange
dog position
now still
she doesn't
know what she
wants

This certainly
be the
letter
I'm being paid
to write

'A' is some
human
letter
that's a start
quotes
like epaulets
on his
shoulders
I hit

a desk &
she's breathing
beneath
me. In
the kitchen
my phone
what should
I write

send off pictures
to everyone
message
for you if you
float
by on your
ship

Aloha

great title!

Television

I guess I'm very attached
to the small boats
moving across the deep
blue sea in a world
much older than ours
but maybe the same
it speaks to me
the smallness
of the boat
the bigness of the night
the shot is wide
and I somehow
feel close
I want to speak
this enormity
to you
I feel like that
or I sing like
that not
modern or loose
at all

I'm loose
like a tiny boat
in a wide cove
opening out into
a bigger body
of water
I relish
the small ripples
like lines that
hold my boat
it's so quiet
in the morning
I imagine myself
seen and what's
seeing me is a for–
lorn love
can you understand
this at all. It's
kind of lost
in a colour
or a tone
something really old
and bound up
with everything
in the moving
picture
and then I
am gone

it changes
into day or
a cartoon
but for the stretch
of that voyage
I am known.

Failed Appointment

if I thought
I couldn't
WRITE
in you
ever
throw her
out. I did.
Time
for something
new. Your
short
broken
self
requires a brand
new
weapon
skinny old
lady
ankles
nobody
sees them
you are

my private
furniture
we're shocked
at her
ass

and a bill
is stuck
to the
wall with
a knife
at least
once we
joked
about piggies
we were
her kids
& pretended
to care
about other
peoples'
hearts.

Notebook, 1981

I was so willing to pull a page out of my notebook, a day, several bright days and live them as if I was only alive, thirsty, timeless, young enough, to do this one more time, to dare to have nothing so much to lose and to feel that potential dying of the self in the light as the only thing I thought that was spiritual, possible and because I had no other way to call that mind, I called it poetry, but it was flesh and time and bread and friends frightened and free enough to want to have another day that way, tear another page.

Kitchen/Holidays

The kettle
whistling
& I'm peeling
an orange
I'm gonna
finish in the
air
of this
wild horn
and I splash
the boiling
water into
the French
press
splattering
water
splashing
grains
I'm such
an oaf
I wanted
to be
here
with you.

In the Picture

someone gave me steroids
& someone gave
me an applause
machine

I cleaned
the mirror
as if I'd
never lived
in evidence
in photographs
I'm the
one who
lives glum

if I'm
happy I
look crazy

stay out of crowds
stay out of photo
graphs

This is not a
good pen
& the car goes
whoosh

get to the airport
early
oops I'm still
shitting

she was in this reading
with us

we would've killed
she did

They'll say *they*
killed.   And

it'll just
be me.

End War

It's a wispy white font
green building
not a poem but a photo
graph
the tree flourishing to its right
tipping to shake and tingle
on the sunny day
I growl at each man
who sat down at my long
table. He climbed up there at night
in wispy script he foretold
a July afternoon in whole foods
was it even here. We fold
our experiences distributing
these words and others
who are also trying to
shake the language tree
receive our letters
and come. I watch
your glowing
backs when you were
young late at night

with lipstick. We shuddered
till you went. Years later
came back selling some
thing. I pick things
up in this room scramble
the words so
their hopeless order
has landed in a comic
book so far away. The violence
of porn. Killing kids.

My Poems

My poems are so much
like the city they
couldn't publish them
on the train

I guess I'm glad
to be back in this relation
ship
it's not my old phone
but it has the same
I just need to be sensitive
to what's riding under
really roiling
the bitch
while I'm riding
on the train.
Nobody knows me
the way my faces change
the vocabulary
of me
if I had a million
stickers

& the date
that poet died
thinking while he lived
he was hitting on students
playing barefoot man
in the winter in a car
If this is my valentine I better also get a treat
there's no news
the whole city thinking
flowers and fruit
I am standing on the
platform a man blows
his nose
he means I love
you. Her boots do. The world
is never superfluous. 2nd
Ave. is just enough.

While You Live Here

after Robin Bruch

Awkward shapes spinning
in green. It's not an
administration it's
a deal. The rusty flag
& a couple of hearts
for you. The friend who
walks barefoot with me
in the night. Because
you're uneven & green
your purple unfolds
like a plan IKEA would
do you no good. Like
blood on a lime green
teevee table. I love you
for the original truth
of inequity, you
are the good govt.
hoeing it alone,
in the thrift shop
you are my patriotism

my resistance to treasure
my acquisition to
pleasure, woman smart
bright boat that
got me home.

Poem at Dusk

Looking
at the tickle
of the leash
of her
body
you stop
and everything
sounds
you lunge
at the flash
of white
further
away. I can't
let you be
wildness
wildness

takes so
long. The drum
in town
is a train
everything's
leaving.

Dear Adam

I said cake

I said top hat

I said microphone

four little golden baby heads

wait I said pirate ghost

wait wait I said closed eye smiling cat

he scrawled back oh my god

I thought fuck yeah I can read this at the marathon

he said Eileen smiles

ehhh I can use it

the bell of my computer rang

same message

wait the cat is crying with relief

the cat is a devil now

the cat is not mad

the cat making racialized jazz

uh or not my white hands

I'm talking to everyone now.

and I'm using a filter. No I'm not

I acknowledge that there is an
image of me twice. I only recently

learned the term jazz hands

if we fucked Pennsylvania up what is our

hope to live in a stolen country that was always stolen

and worked largely by stolen people. Out of a
    conservative

diaspora came I mongrel poet from Massachusetts

to make my mark

love & these things and opportunities

to speak. We can't fall down we teem in the new
    opportunity
we discover what resistance means

our time & blowing up the inside of my computer

buck studies

the phone says delivered

what is.

Adam says did you see my beard.

We talk about money awhile

I ride my bike. Get off the phone goes
ding. It's his beard calling. I go oh.

you have what I want.

he says lol

then skull

then rocket

then turkey

green pistol

and a flame. I

don't know what to say back to that

I say bike and go.

A Little Bit

It's a little bit
true that the
hole in my jacket
pocket
the breast pocket
yeah all relaxed
has a hole &
pens keep
slipping through
one's in the lining
but this one
perched
now it's a writing
bird
silly black out there
wants to
tell its
song. Manuel's
book was
in the air &
I was on

a train
my feet are cold
and you wouldn't
be in the
air so
long it doesn't happen
like this
there's no climate
in a plane
and I was in one
but not on
earth
my mother
is gone
each thing I do
is a little
bit wrong. I'm willing
to apologize
but they never
help it's
just pointing
out the hole
& people
forget but I
won't forget
you

The West

There might be nothing
the section of the paper
I save for later
about buildings, the
home, inside.
Outside too. *Yard*
The garden. Things that do
well. What I have in mind.
My favorite
radio show is garden
compass. It's like gossip
about someone else's
life and how
to save them and their
plants and their
flowers. It's like Heloise
the road is long
I mean it. All I need
is to hear a certain
designer plans
to be alone for the rest
of his life and I

think I'm like him.
And I'm dying to see
that movie
how he does
every little thing.
It's as simple as being
a sculpture, having
a life. This is not the book
of instruction I had intended
but this is
when the emptiness noticed
its own beginning like
that church I saw when
I was young
that was simply melting
This is for those who
would not name
that building. But simply
step in, noticing
when that has happened
an elaborate piece
like being a candelabra
that that is the road
you are on. I thought bring
your camera. I thought
don't bring your camera
that's what I mean.
There will be plenty for everyone
and my style is adequate

to that. Has been planning
this moment for years.
Ushering it in. Tonight I will do
books. I am leaving my house.
Which ones do I need
I think *you* can come
on the long & horizontal road of reading.

The Vow

Everything's like a shade
of brightness and dark
like this new pad
I got
or my computer
or these doorways opening
one to the next
which is where I
began. Nothing is like
my dog eating an
apple core in bed
The sleeping
bag is read. It's March
and it's already
warm. I don't want
you stepping on
my computer which is
where all my friends
are some of whom are Nazis
I never thought I'd call Nazis
friends but I spend
at least an hour

a night w these ones &
then I wake up
and read about
the real ones on
Twitter. For days Rebecca
Solnit
& I struggled to be
facebook friends.
It was like we were
going to the gym
together. We worked
it out. I was visiting
her today looking
at her face. The heat
just rumbled. It's not
even evening but I
thought I'd get
a little nazi
in early. I would die
for my country
if that included
everything, my friends,
and my dogs
and all the lakes
and ponds. I
am ready
for the struggle.

creep

ugly nightmare
eating too much
dunking your head in water
over and over
again. Feel bad
for your kid
all of them
but most of all us
bad nights
when I was young
and drinking pred
atory men
with swollen
heads would
buy me drinks
and want to fuck
me again &
again because
I was nothing
to them and he is
our president
now.

Transmission

I'm overcome
by the cruelty
of nature
no I mean
I'm with
it. And each
little capacity
it has
can't be transferred
I mean
a spruce
can't give
its oils to you
can it.
But that's how
it grows
in the ab
sence of
technology
my thoughts
grow. My thoughts
grow among

trees
but I don't
help them
though
I'm for them.
I'm for my
dog & inci
dentally
I feed
her but I
don't see
her much.
Joe does.
Joe is
my friend
& also
a dog father
I don't
help mountains
Mountains
help me
I know
the planet
is old
& splashy
sleep helps
me. Time
helps
me. My mother

helped
me. And
now she
is gone. She
also hurt
me so it's
good that
she's gone.
I can grow
different
in the
day or
three decades
in which
I've got
left
I can
grow towards
the mountains
sit in solidarity
with prisoners
or go
to jail. I'm not joking
I can
push different.
I want
to say
something
about my cunt.

Because
That's
what you
ask. But
I am
alone. No
mother
no phone
just a notebook
& a cunt
& my thoughts.
I don't
even think
my thoughts.
you do.

A hundred per cent

I would like
a century
a tree
grows slow
a crack
of light
hits my palm
while I'm
reading
I grab
to take
a picture
& the crack
is gone
branches
pouring
out of my
hands
days has made
its mark
I have
wind

swept
hair I think
of my step
brother
who I knew
more
like this
his face
a photo
graph
on a beach
on a
book &
when he died
I was
family
watching
a tree in
the wind
& I wanted
to speak
to him
who was
truly my
brother
that speck
of light is gone
on my
hand and

him. I told
her I'd probably
like to
end here
like my com
puters
do & my
dog did. I took
a chance
w horrifying
her. I'm
shooting
for this
love where
I live. See
me dying
now or running
across
the beach
to catch
the tree
book
cover in the end
of summer's
wind. The ocean
is a feast
& it's here
I bring my
water tree book

feet, taste
branches
the lot that
is me
who wants
a century.

Sweet heart

Fresca's got a new look
but I'm not drinking
that. My coke
struck the ice
and the ice
cube cracked.
I'm sitting by the little
Buddha
who is sitting in
my yard. I imagine
you walking in
gasping at the
same couch
the same bed
it's almost
the same
town but this is
what I meant
and there's
so much pleasure,
difference in
this, that. I <u>meant</u>

to be here. One
sleeps on what
they mean
and arises on the decided
side and that's
the hope. An entire
room is opened
by particular feelings
that say you're
on the edge
of the space
and then you
wait to watch
it grow. Grow
like a love
or a feeling of distrust
or a body grateful
for sun & breeze
and the rising and
falling of my dog's
chest no gut.
The little Buddha's
smiling southeast
I figured that
out. Their
genitals are
unknown in fact
their everything's
smiling walked on

by ants planted
in the dirt
but not dead
activated by my
gaze. Their smiling
makes me glad
dog turns buddha's
way I go
forward with con
fidence I
may turn nothing
up but this
gentle scratching
in my yard
before making
a call opening
the self
somehow so it's
possible to
have a friend
to call
not only from
need but interest
in their life
the body I'm
pouring into
joyous to be
connected
to someone

while covered
by ants surrounded
by breeze
actually touched
by birds
their sound
then landing
there is nothing
romantic
in their
absence
the bird
is all touch
no matter
how distant
their flight
the sky is open
my gaze is
wide it matters
how they
dive and
hover. The silly
cluck the ninny
constant
the hoot makes
the grey sky
blue; trees
brown; green
slanting trees

the woman
dying in her
face thought
am I recording
but it was
the young man
counting everything
Korakrit
whose art
I liked
so much
performed bird
in the dying
woman's sky
so his
quote was reverential
that she
could be copying
anything by
dying was more about
him. A moustache
on the sound
that life's
made
of. I think
you don't
miss me
enough
or you regard

me as seasons
that simply
come & it's
true I'm
everything. I used
to love
so much
to show
you
my
poems.
but everything's
not enough
you have to go out
& shake
everything's
hand and the
tremendous
feeling of
everything
is not shook enough.
I'm sick of being
god for you.
I'm not the
Fresca or
the Buddha
or the bird. I'm
the ice
that cracks

I'm really
feeling it
now. The amazing
difference
of contact
everything's
gasp. It begins
so slow. Hours
of freezing waiting
a life
and the draining
of it
by waiting
too long. Riding
around in
a car. I'm not
any coke. I'm
every
coke. And
a bird
likes the
sound of
that: to be
so close
the earth
parts for
its own
arrival. The time
of day

is enchanted
by my jeans
on the line.
I'm enchanted
by everything
too. How could
I be it
and feel it.
Drawing sun lines
sticks.
If I say too
again and
I'm creating
a pattern
someone who
doesn't love
me will
say you
say too too
much. I suppose
going blind is momentarily
seeing colors
in everything
and remembering
them for
the rest of
your life. I'm afraid
to tell you I'm
going blind. What

I'm saying
is I'm retiring
from god. I will
feel my genius
quietly the furrows
of a dead
tree accepting
my love. You start
like a car
and pepper
in a number
of growls. That's dog.
you roll
and you're
bird and
Buddha's
difficult
now. More
of an
aside. That something
so different
as the sun
could turn
I think
and we're turning
on our dirty
little urn
there's a movie
about everything

my getting
this part
of that
endlessly
obliged
to be wise. Upstairs
16 little
eggs turn
in another
galaxy someone
else's sandwich.
Today I
was so busy
I didn't
even see
lunch. I had
it but
I didn't
see it
at all. The distant
eggs are turning
for someone
else. I poured
Fresca
into my glass
and then
I poured
my vodka
and then

I got drunk.
Darker
day now
when my throat
fills and
Buddha's
awake. A bee
wants
to sting
me and
in that
moment
I would
notice
everything. Why
do you
think I'm
sweet. Why
must I
die.

acknowledgments

Some of these poems have appeared in the following publications: *BOMB*; *Tender Journal*; *Hyperallergic*; *St. Petersburg Review*; *Atlas Review*; *Troubling the Line: Trans and Genderqueer Poetry and Poetics*; *Critical Quarterly*; *A Public Space*; *EOAGH*; *Re-Edition Magazine*; Poem-a-Day from the Academy of American Poets; *Poetry*; *Prairie Schooner*; *Jubilat*; *The American Reader*; *Future Perfect Magazine*; *T, The New York Times Style Magazine*; *Prelude*; *Privacy Policy: The Anthology of Surveillance Poetics*; *Dancers, Buildings and People in the Streets: Danspace Project Platform*; *Green Mountains Review*; *The Best American Poetry 2013*; *The Best of the Lifted Brow*, Vol. 2 and *The Lifted Brow*, Issue 25; *New Yorker*; *Artforum*; *No Prizes*; *Document Journal*; *Literary Hub*; *WORD: An Anthology by A Gathering of the Tribes*; *Harper's*; *Paris Review*; *Cambridge Literary Review*; *Helen Marten: Drunk Brown House*; *Aphros*; *New York Review of Books*; *Grey Book*; Jason Dodge's *Fivehundred Places*; *A Restricted View from Under the Hedge*; *Weekday*; *Blau Magazin*; *Resistance, Rebellion, Life: 50 Poems Now*; *Resist Much, Obey Little: Inaugural Poems to the Resistance*; and *Love's Executive Order*.

I'd like to thank each of these editors for their brilliance and their generosity.

I want to thank everyone at Grove for being the absolute greatest and in particular my editor, soul mate, friend Zach Pace. PJ Mark, always the best imaginable and more. I want to thank the

MacDowell Colony, that makes writing home, Lannan Foundation, especially Martha Jessup, and my warm growing Marfa life, NYU Creative Writing, Lacy Schutz and the Shaker Museum, PalFest, Foundation for Contemporary Art travel grant, Anna Halberstadt, the Ukrainian Literary Center, Jill Soloway truly, Zoe Leonard for being great and a great invite, Natalie Diaz for receiving a poem and writing one, Daniella Shreir for vision at the nick of time, so too Erin Kimmel, all style, and Adam of course but I already said that. Erica Kaufman, genius, Porochista thanks for your honest mind. Everyone else thank you thank you and hi.